52 more Weeks of Family Night

of Family Night

SCRIPTURE STUDY EDITION

52 more Weeks of Family Night

SCRIPTURE STUDY EDITION

DIANE KIRKPATRICK

Covenant Communications, Inc.

Cover image: *Smiling Family of Five Holding Together* © Iva Villi. Courtesy of Shutterstock.com.

Cover design copyrighted 2010 by Covenant Communications, Inc.

Published by Covenant Communications, Inc.

American Fork, Utah

Copyright © 2010 by Diane Kirkpatrick

Printed in the United States of America

First Printing: January 2010

15 14 13 12 11 10   10 9 8 7 6 5 4 3 2 1

ISBN 978-1-59811-978-7

Contents

How to Use This Book

This book is set up so families with young children can enjoy the blessings of family night and daily scripture study. There is no right or wrong way to use this book. There are 52 topics, one for each week of the year. Topics do not need to be read in order. Use them however you wish. You may print the activities from the CD-ROM as many times as you'd like, and mix and match them to suit your family's situation.

This book includes the following for each topic:

- suggested music from the LDS hymnbook *(Hymns)* and the *Children's Songbook*
- a scripture to memorize
- five suggested scriptures relating to the topic

- questions about those scriptures
- an icon that indicates the type of activity that will be found on the CD-ROM.

The downloadable CD-ROM includes the following:
- a large-type version of the scripture to be memorized
- five activities such as mazes, crossword puzzles, word searches, word scrambles, scripture scrambles
- talk and journal suggestions for each topic

Here are a few suggestions for how this book can be used:

Family night lessons. Choose a topic for your FHE. Use the recommended music. Practice the scripture memorization. Read some or all of the scriptures and do all or some of the activities.

Daily scripture study. Choose one of the 52 scripture topics and print the memory verse at the beginning of the week. Each day read the scripture verse for that day, ask questions about the verse, and use the associated activity to learn about the chosen topic.

Do a combination. Do the daily scripture reading followed or preceded by a Family Home Evening about the topic.

For instructions on how to use the CD-ROM, see p. 117.

The icons in this book

 *Categorize*

 *Crossword*

⭐ *Decoding*

✏️ *Fill-in-the-blank*

🔄 *Matching*

▦ *Maze*

⚡ *Memory verse*

📋 *Missing letters*

📖 *Scripture scramble*

🔤 *Word scramble*

🔍 *Word search*

•1•
Agency

"Choose the Right" (*Hymns,* 239)
"Choose the Right Way" (*Children's Songbook,* 160)

✡ *Scripture memory: 2 Nephi 2:16*

⟳ *Activity 1: 2 Nephi 2:15–16*
- What do you need in order to make a choice? You need things to choose between. Each choice needs to be desirable.
- What is the opposite of the forbidden fruit? The tree of life.
- Are we allowed to act for ourselves? Yes.

❓ *Activity 2: 2 Nephi 2:27*
- What are the two choices? Liberty and life or captivity and death.
- Who is miserable? Satan.
- What does Satan want you to choose? Sin and death, just as he did.

• How do you choose liberty and eternal life? By choosing to keep the commandments and repenting if you make mistakes.

 Activity 3: Helaman 14:30
• Can we blame other people for our actions? No.
• What knowledge makes us free? To know good from evil.

Activity 4: D&C 29:36
• Did we have agency before we were born? Yes. We were allowed to choose to follow Satan or God in the premortal world.
• Who did you choose to follow? You chose to follow God because you are here on earth now.

Activity 5: Moses 4:3
• What did Satan want to destroy? God's plan of happiness by taking away man's agency.
• Where is Satan now because of that? He is cast down.
• How do we know agency is a great gift? Because God cast out Satan for wanting to destroy it.

•2•
Assurance

"I Stand All Amazed" (*Hymns*, 193)
"He Sent His Son" (*Children's Songbook*, 34)

📖 *Scripture memory: D&C 19:16*

🔳 *Activity 1: John 6:33; 14:27*
- What is the peace Christ speaks of? It is a feeling of calm assurance, safety, and love.
- Have you ever felt this peace?

🔁 *Activity 2: Isaiah 9:6*
- Why is Christ called the Prince of Peace? He gives us peace if we ask Him. He will rule the world during the Millennium when there will be peace. He sends us peace after we have repented.

🔲 *Activity 3: Mosiah 4:3*
- How did the people feel peace in their hearts? They had peace of conscience.

- Why did they have a peace of conscience? Their sins had been forgiven.

- Why were they filled with joy? They experienced the love of Jesus Christ.

🔤 Activity 4: Alma 58:10–12

- When the war wasn't going well, what did the Nephites do? They prayed.

- What happened after they prayed? They felt assurance, faith, and hope.

- How can you feel hope and peace during your trials? By praying to God.

⭐ Activity 5: Helaman 5:42–47

- Where were Nephi and Lehi? They were in a Lamanite prison.

- What did they hear? A voice.

- How did the voice sound? It was still and small but very powerful.

- What did the voice tell them? "Peace be unto you because of your faith."

- We can have peace in our hearts if we have faith in the Peacegiver.

•3•
Atonement

"Master, the Tempest Is Raging" (Hymns,)
"I Feel My Savior's Love" (Children's Songbook, 74)

 *Scripture memory: John 14:27*

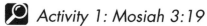 *Activity 1: Mosiah 3:19*

- What is the natural man? He is an enemy to God.

- Why is he an enemy? Because he doesn't want to obey the commandments.

- How do you overcome the natural man? By listening to the Holy Spirit.

- What does the Holy Spirit tell you to do? Be humble, patient, and loving.

- Who needs the Atonement? Everyone, because we all need to overcome the natural man.

Activity 2: D&C 19:16–19

- Why did Jesus suffer? So we could repent and be redeemed.

- What was His suffering like? It was almost too much for Him to bear.
- What happens if we don't take advantage of the Atonement by repenting? We have to suffer as Jesus did.

❓ Activity 3: Alma 34:14–17
- What overpowers justice? The atonement and suffering of Jesus Christ.
- When does mercy overpower justice? When we have faith and call on His name.
- What is meant by an infinite and eternal sacrifice? Its blessings are available to everyone in every time.

📖 Activity 4: 2 Nephi 9:6–10
- If we didn't have the Atonement and the Resurrection, who would we have to obey? Satan.
- Why is the great plan of the Creator so merciful? Because in spite of our mistakes, we can be resurrected, and we can be forgiven of our sins.

📋 Activity 5: D&C 74:7
- Is there hope for people who do not hear the gospel during their lifetimes? Yes, those who didn't know the law are covered by the Atonement.
- Can little children sin? No. They are innocent, and the Atonement covers them.

•4•
Baptism

"Come, Follow Me" (Hymns, 116)
"When Jesus Christ Was Baptized" (Children's Songbook, 102)

 Scripture memory: 3 Nephi 11:33

 Activity 1: 2 Nephi 9:23–24

• Who must repent? All men.

• According to this scripture, what are four things we need to do? Repent, believe, be baptized, and endure to the end.

• Why are we baptized? To show our obedience and to join Christ's Church.

Activity 2: D&C 20:72–74; D&C 76:51

• Who has to have authority from God? The person who baptizes you.

• How is baptism done? By immersing the person in the water after saying the words of the baptismal prayer.

10

• Why is the person immersed in the water? Because it is a commandment, it symbolizes how Jesus was once buried and now is resurrected, and Jesus was baptized by immersion.

 Activity 3: 2 Nephi 31:17–18

• What is the gate? Repentance and baptism.

• Where does the gate lead? To the strait and narrow path leading to eternal life.

• What gift do you receive after you enter the gate? The Holy Ghost.

 Activity 4: Joseph Smith–History 1:68–71

• After Joseph Smith and Oliver Cowdery went to the woods to pray about baptism, what happened? An angel came and gave them the priesthood of Aaron, which gave them the authority to baptize.

• What did the angel command them to do? To ordain and then baptize each other.

⭐ *Activity 5: John 3:3–5*

• What does it mean to be born again? To have a clean, fresh start in life.

How are you born of the water and the Spirit? By being baptized.

•5•
Brotherhood

"Love One Another" (*Hymns*, 308)
"Friends Are Fun" (*Children's Songbook*, 262)

Scripture memory: 3 Nephi 14:12

Activity 1: 1 Samuel 20:41–42

• Jonathan was King Saul's son. David was appointed to be the next king. Jonathan and David should have been rivals. Did they act like it? No. They were good friends.

• What kind of oath did they swear? An oath of friendship.

Activity 2: Ruth 1:8–17

• Naomi had two sons who were married to Orpah and Ruth. When her sons died, she tried to send her daughters-in-law back to their homes, which were in other lands. Orpah left; what did Ruth do? She stayed with Naomi.

• How do we know Naomi and Ruth loved each other? They stayed together and helped each other.

• How should you treat your friends? Help them, be loyal to them, and spend time with them.

 Activity 3: Alma 17:2–3

• Alma had been good friends with the sons of Mosiah. They were together when they saw the angel who called them to repentance. They didn't see each other for a long time. What did Alma do when he finally saw his brethren again? He rejoiced exceedingly.

• What added more to his joy? That they were all still strong in the gospel.

• What is so special about friends who share your beliefs? You can strengthen each other and your testimonies.

 Activity 4: D&C 135:3

• What was the relationship between Joseph and Hyrum? They were brothers.

• How do we know they were also friends? They helped each other and loved each other.

• Our brothers and sisters can be some of our best friends. How should we treat our brothers and sisters? Help them and be nice to them. Be loyal to them.

 Activity 5: D&C 108:7

• What should you do for your friends? Strengthen them.

• How do you strengthen your friends? By praying for them, encouraging them, and helping them.

•6•
Charity

"A Poor Wayfaring Man of Grief" (*Hymns*, 29)
"Jesus Said Love Everyone" (*Children's Songbook*, 61)

📷 *Scripture memory: Moroni 7:47*

❓ *Activity 1: Moroni 7:45–47*
- What is charity? The pure love of Christ.
- What are some words used to describe charity? Patient, hopeful, truth-loving, innocent, enduring.

⭐ *Activity 2: Alma 7:24*
- If you have charity, what will you do? Good works.
- Why will you do good works if you have charity? Because you will want to show others how much you love them.

🧩 *Activity 3: Luke 10:30–37*
- Who did not show charity for the wounded man? The Levite and the priest.

- Who showed charity toward the wounded man? The Samaritan.

- How did he show charity? He helped the wounded man.

Activity 4: Matthew 5:43–44

- Should you hate your enemies? No. You should love them and pray for them.

- Charity means loving those who aren't easy to love.

Activity 5: Ether 12:33–34

- How do we know Jesus had charity? He gave his life for us because He loved us.

- Who needs to have charity? Everyone.

- What happens if we don't have charity? We can't live with Heavenly Father.

•7•
Christmas
(Book of Mormon)

"Joy to the World" (*Hymns*, 201)
"Samuel Tells of the Baby Jesus" (*Children's Songbook*, 36)

🔖 *Scripture memory: 3 Nephi 1:13*

🔲 *Activity 1: Mosiah 3:1–8*

• An angel told King Benjamin about Jesus many years before Jesus was born. What did the angel tell King Benjamin about Jesus? He would be born, His mother's name would be Mary, He would do miracles, He would die for the sins of the world, and He would be resurrected.

• What is a tabernacle of clay? It is a mortal body.

🔲 *Activity 2: 3 Nephi 1:4–9*

• Just before Christ was to be born, the righteous

Nephites were looking forward to a sign. What was the sign supposed to be? A night where there would be no darkness.

- If the sign didn't appear at a certain time, what would happen to the faithful? The unbelievers would put them to death.

🔣✎ Activity 3: 3 Nephi 1:15–21

- Were the signs fulfilled among the Nephites? Yes.
- What were the signs? The night was not dark, and a new star appeared.
- Did everyone know this was the sign of Jesus' birth? Yes, and some people got very nervous about it.

🔤 Activity 4: 2 Nephi 9:21–22

- Why are we so happy that Jesus was born? He would save all men from endless torment and from death.
- Who is He going to save? He will save men, women, and children.

⭐ Activity 5: Mosiah 2:17

- What gift can we give to Jesus on His birthday? We can serve others, because when we serve others we serve God.

•8•
Christmas
(New Testament)

Christmas carols (*Hymns, 201–204*)
Christmas section (*Children's Songbook, 36–52*)

 *Scripture memory: Luke 2:11*

📖 *Activity 1: Luke 1:26–38*
- Who came to talk to Mary? Angel Gabriel.
- What did the angel tell her? That she would have a son, and He would be Jesus, the savior of the world.
- What did Mary tell the angel? That she would be obedient.

📋 *Activity 2: Luke 1:39–45*
- Who also testified about Jesus? Elisabeth, Mary's cousin, knew Mary would give birth to Jesus because her own baby leapt in her womb.

• What did Elisabeth call Mary? Blessed among women.

🔎 Activity 3: Luke 2:1–7

• Why did Joseph and Mary travel out of Galilee to Bethlehem? Because they had to be taxed in the city of their ancestors.

• Why did Mary lay Jesus in a manger? There was no room for her and Joseph in the inn.

⟳📝 Activity 4: Luke 2:8–20

• How did the shepherds learn about Jesus' birth? The angels told them.

• What did they do after the angels left? They went to find the baby.

• What did the shepherds do after they saw the babe? They told others, and they glorified God.

❓ Activity 5: Matthew 2:1–12

• Who came to worship Jesus? Wise men from the East.

• How did they find him? They followed the star.

• What did the Wise Men bring to Jesus? Gold, frankincense, and myrrh.

• Did they tell Herod where Jesus was? No. They were warned in a dream to stay away from the wicked ruler.

•9•
Creation

"All Creatures of Our God and King" (*Hymns*, 62)
"All Things Bright and Beautiful" (*Children's Songbook*, 231)

 *Scripture memory: Genesis 1:1*

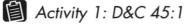 *Activity 1: D&C 45:1*

- What did God create? The heavens, the earth, and all the hosts of earth.
- Who are the hosts of earth? Anything that lives, moves, or has being—people, plants, and animals.

Activity 2: Genesis 1:1–13

- What did God create on the first day? Day and night.
- What did God create on the second day? Firmament and water.
- What did God create on the third day? Dry land and seas.

🔍 *Activity 3: Genesis 1:14–23*

- What did God create on the fourth day? The sun, moon, and stars.
- What did God create on the fifth day? Sea life and birds.

↩📝 *Activity 4: Genesis 1:24–31*

- What did God create on the sixth day? Animals and man.
- What did God create man to resemble? His own image.
- What commandment did He give Adam and Eve? To multiply and replenish the earth.

❓ *Activity 5: Moses 6:63; Alma 30:43–44*

- What bears record of God? All things, spiritual and temporal, heavenly and on earth.
- Did Korihor believe in God? No.
- What did he want in order to believe that God existed? He wanted a sign.
- Alma told him he already had signs enough. What were they? The testimonies of the scriptures and prophets and all the creations.

•10•
Dependability

"True to the Faith" (*Hymns,* 254)
"When We're Helping" (*Children's Songbook,* 198)

 Scripture memory: Alma 53:20

 Activity 1: 1 Nephi 2:8–10
- What did Lehi want Laman to be like? A river.
- What did Lehi want Lemuel to be like? A valley.
- Why did he want them to be like a river and a valley? Because rivers and valleys don't change easily. They are dependable.
- What does it mean to be dependable? That you can be counted on. You will always do you what you have promised.

Activity 2: 1 Nephi 3:7
- How did Nephi show that he was dependable? He would go and do whatever the Lord commanded him.
- Would Nephi give up if it got too hard? No. Nephi

knew the Lord would help him even if the commandment was hard to keep.

- Could the Lord depend on Nephi? Yes.
- Can the Lord depend on you?

🔤 Activity 3: Alma 53:20

- Who were these young men? They were the stripling warriors.
- How were they dependable? They were true at all times to whatever was entrusted to them.
- Why do good warriors need to be dependable? They need to follow all of their captain's orders, or they can't win a battle.

❓ Activity 4: Alma 39:1–4

- What was Corianton supposed to be doing? Serving a mission.
- Did he do what he was supposed to do? No. He got distracted by other things.
- Was Corianton dependable? No. He didn't do his assigned job.

⭐ Activity 5: 2 Nephi 27:23

- Does God ever change? No. He is the same yesterday, today, and forever.
- Can we depend on Him to be there to help us? He will always help us. God is dependable so we should be too.

•11•
Education

"Oh Say, What Is Truth?" (Hymns, 272)
"Teach Me to Walk in the Light" (Children's Songbook, 177)

 Scripture memory: D&C 88:118

 Activity 1: D&C 93:36
- What is the glory of God? Intelligence.
- What does that mean? It is good to be intelligent; it glorifies God.
- What is light and truth? Intelligence.
- How can we become more intelligent? By studying, thinking, and praying.

Activity 2: Matthew 25:1–13
- Why didn't the virgins share their oil? They couldn't share because they needed it. You can't give someone a testimony, and you can't give someone your education.
- To become more spiritual, what do you think the wise

virgins did? Prayed, served, studied hard, and kept the commandments.

• What do you think the foolish virgins failed to do? They didn't take the commandments seriously, they didn't care, and they didn't try.

Activity 3: D&C 88:118

• Where should you seek wisdom? Out of the best books.

• What are the best books? The scriptures and other well-written, truthful books.

• Besides study, what is one way to learn? Faith.

• Why do you need faith to learn? You need to have faith that learning will be good for you, that God will help you understand things.

Activity 4: D&C 130:18–19

• Will intelligence help us in the next life? Yes. You can take that with you when you die.

• What will not help you in the next life? Riches, fame, popularity.

• Why should we try to learn while we are in this life? Because we will have a much greater advantage later on.

Activity 5: 2 Nephi 9:28–29

• If you learn many things in this life, what do you have to be careful of? Thinking you know it all.

- What do learned people sometimes forget? Sometimes really learned people forget they need to depend on God. They think they are so smart they don't need Him.

•12•
Endurance

"Carry On" (*Hymns*, 255)
"Dare to Do Right" (*Children's Songbook*, 158)

 Scripture memory: D&C 121:7–8

 Activity 1: 2 Nephi 31:15

• How do endurance runners compete? They run for a long time instead of short distances.

• What does it mean to endure? To make it to the end of the race or of this life.

• Would someone who endures give up? No. He or she would keep going, no matter what.

 Activity 2: Mosiah 23:20–24

• How did the people in Helam behave? They were righteous.

• Did the Lord save them from trials? No. Their patience had to be tried.

• Did their trials make them sad or make them want to

give up? No. They rejoiced because God delivered them after their sufferings.

Activity 3: D&C 121:1–8

- This is a prayer said by Joseph Smith while he was in Liberty Jail. What was Joseph Smith asking for? He wanted the persecutions to stop. He wanted to know how much longer they would have to suffer.
- How did God answer Joseph's prayer? He was given peace.
- How do you endure well? You don't complain, you rely on God for strength.

Activity 4: 2 Nephi 31:19–20

- What is the gate? Baptism.
- What does the gate lead to? The strait and narrow path.
- Does baptism assure you eternal life? No. You also have to endure to the end.

Activity 5: D&C 14:7

- What is a reward for enduring to the end? Eternal life.
- What is the greatest gift of God? Eternal life.

•13•
Eternal Families

"Love at Home" (*Hymns,* 294)
"Families Can Be Together Forever" (*Children's Songbook,* 188)

🔖 *Scripture memory: The Family: A Proclamation to the World, paragraph 1*

❓ *Activity 1: First and second paragraphs*
- What is central to Heavenly Father's plan for His children? The family.
- What is ordained of God? Marriage between a man and a woman.

🔍 *Activity 2: Third paragraph*
- When did we agree to Heavenly Father's plan? Before we were born.
- Can the family continue after the grave? Yes, through sacred ordinances.

- What makes it possible for families to be reunited after the grave? Temple ordinances.

⛊ Activity 3: Sixth paragraph
- What is the duty of a husband and wife? To take care of their children physically and spiritually.
- What should they teach their children? To love and serve each other, to obey the commandments, and to be good citizens.

❓ Activity 4: Seventh paragraph
- A happy family is founded on what? The teachings of Jesus Christ.
- Successful families practice what principles? Faith, prayer, repentance, forgiveness, respect, love, compassion, work, and wholesome recreational activities.

🔠 Activity 5: Eighth paragraph
- What happens if you don't fulfill your family responsibilities? You will have to answer to God.
- What will bring on the calamities foretold by ancient and modern prophets? The disintegration of the family.

•14•
Example

"The Lord Is My Light" (*Hymns,* 89)
"I'm Trying to Be like Jesus" (*Children's Songbook,* 78)

 *Scripture memory: Matthew 5:14*

Activity 1: Matthew 5:14–16

- In what way are you the light of the world? Because you are an example to others.
- Who can see the candle? The whole house can see it.
- Who does your example affect? All those who see it.

Activity 2: John 13:14–16

- How did Jesus teach His disciples? He taught them by example.
- What did Jesus do? He washed their feet.
- What did Jesus expect the disciples to do? To serve each other.
- Since Jesus served others, what should we do? Serve others as well.

Activity 3: Alma 39:1, 11

- Who set a good example? Helaman, because of his faithfulness.

- Who did not set a good example? Corianton, because of his iniquity.

- What happened because Corianton was not a good example? Many people would not believe his testimony of the gospel.

 Activity 4: 1 Nephi 7:8

- Who was the good example? Nephi was a good example to his brothers.

- Do you have to be old to be a good example? No. Anyone can be a good example. Nephi was the younger brother.

- How are you a good example in your family?

 Activity 5: 2 Nephi 31:12–13

- Whose example should we follow? Jesus Christ's example.

- How should we follow Him? With full purpose of heart.

- What did He do that we should follow? Pray, serve, love, be baptized, receive the Holy Ghost.

•15•
Faith

"I Know That My Redeemer Lives" (*Hymns,* 136)
"Faith" (*Children's Songbook,* 96)

 *Scripture memory: Alma 32:21*

Activity 1: Alma 32:17–21

• Is faith a perfect knowledge? No. It is hope for things not seen that are true.

• What is perfect knowledge? You have seen and you know for sure.

• Can you have faith in things that are not true? No. They must be true.

• If you see a sign, do you develop faith? No, because now you know for sure.

Activity 2: Alma 32:27–29

• What is the experiment? To see if you can develop faith.

- Do you need faith to begin with? No. You only need to desire to believe.
- What is the seed? The word of God.
- How do you know if the seed is good? You begin to feel happy, to understand, and your doubts go away.

🔍 Activity 3: Ether 3:3–10

- What did the Brother of Jared ask the Lord to do? To touch the stones and make them shine in the darkness.
- What did the Brother of Jared see? He saw the Lord's finger.
- How was the Brother of Jared able to see the finger? Because he had such great faith.

▦ Activity 4: John 20:24–29

- Who visited the disciples? Jesus.
- Who was missing the first time Jesus came? Thomas.
- When did Thomas say he would believe? When he could see Jesus for himself.
- Who is more blessed? Those who have not seen yet believe.

📋 Activity 5: Ether 12:6

- When do you see a witness? After the trial of your faith.
- What is faith? Things hoped for, but not seen.
- Should you dispute if you don't have proof? No.

•16•
Family History

"Turn Your Hearts" (*Hymns*, 291)
"Truth from Elijah" (*Children's Songbook*, 90)

 Scripture memory: D&C 2:2

📖 *Activity 1: D&C 2*

• How do the hearts of the children turn to their fathers? The children do family history work, including genealogy and temple work.

• What are the promises made to the fathers? That we will seek them out and perform their temple work.

• If the children and the fathers were to fail to turn to each other, what would happen? The earth would be wasted.

• Why would the earth be wasted? Those who came to live here would be without the gospel and its eternal blessings.

⭐ *Activity 2: D&C 110:13–16*

• Who appeared to Joseph Smith? Elijah.

• What did Elijah bring? The keys to seal families together.

• Had Elijah's visit been expected? It had been prophesied he would restore the keys before the great and dreadful day of the Lord.

✎ Activity 3: Mosiah 1:6–7
• What did the plates of Nephi contain? Records and sayings of their fathers—the Nephites' history.

• What would happen if the people searched plates? They would profit or benefit from them because of what they can learn.

❓ Activity 4: Mosiah 27:13–16
• What did the angel tell Alma? He told him to stop persecuting the saints.

• Why was Alma asked to remember the people of Helam, who were his ancestors? Because they had been delivered from bondage. Alma could learn from their faith to have faith also.

• Why are the faith-promoting stories of our parents and ancestors so important? We can learn from their struggles and triumphs.

🔍 Activity 5: Alma 9:6–11
• Was there only one man declaring the gospel to the

people in Ammonihah? No. Many had preached to them and there had been many miracles among them.

- If we write about our testimonies and spiritual experiences, who could be helped? Our children.

- How will that be helpful? They can gain faith from our testimonies.

•17•
Fasting

"In Fasting We Approach Thee" (*Hymns,* 139)
"I Know My Father Lives" (*Children's Songbook,* 5)

 Scripture memory: D&C 59:13

 Activity 1: Alma 17:3

• Why were the sons of Mosiah able to teach with power? They fasted and prayed much.

• How did they get the spirit of prophecy and revelation? By fasting and praying.

• How can you gain the spirit of prophecy and revelation? By fasting and praying.

Activity 2: Mosiah 27:21–23

• When the people saw that Alma couldn't move or speak, what did they do? They fasted and prayed for his recovery.

• Did their fasting and prayer work? Yes. After two days, he regained his strength.

? *Activity 3: Matthew 6:16–18*

• How do hypocrites fast? They make sure everyone knows they are suffering.

• How should you fast? You should wash and be happy and not show suffering.

• If you fast in secret, how will you be rewarded? Openly.

▦ *Activity 4: Isaiah 58:3–11*

• These people were fasting for the wrong reasons. What were these reasons? For strife and to be seen of others.

• What are you supposed to do? Help those who are hungry, not just suffer hunger yourself.

• What are some rewards of fasting? Health and prosperity as well as spiritual fulfillment.

★ *Activity 5: D&C 59:13–16*

• How should we fast? With a joyful heart and countenance.

• What are the rewards for this? The "fulness" of the earth.

•18•
Forgiveness

"Lord, I Would Follow Thee" (*Hymns*, 220)
"Help Me, Dear Father" (*Children's Songbook*, 99)

Scripture memory: D&C 64:9

Activity 1: 3 Nephi 13:14–15
- Who does Heavenly Father expect you to forgive? Everyone.
- What if you don't forgive? Then you won't be forgiven.

Activity 2: D&C 64: 8–9
- Who has the greater sin? The one who does not forgive.
- What happened to the disciples who did not forgive? They were chastened.
- Who are you required to forgive? All men.

Activity 3: Luke 15:11–32
- What happened to the prodigal son? He spent all his money in riotous living but then repented and came home.

- How did his father treat him? He forgave him and celebrated his homecoming with a big feast.

 ### *Activity 4: Enos 1:4–8*
- What did Enos pray for? He prayed for his own soul.
- What did the Lord tell him? That his sins were forgiven.
- What did Enos ask? How is it done? How could he be forgiven?
- How is forgiveness achieved? Through faith in the atonement of Jesus Christ.

Activity 5: Matthew 18:21–35
- What did Peter ask the Lord? How many times he had to forgive.
- How many times did the Lord say Peter needed to forgive? Seventy times seven times.
- How many times do you need to forgive? Every time you are asked.
- Did the king forgive the person who owed him ten thousand talents? Yes, because he asked him.
- Did the servant forgive the person who owed him one hundred pence? No.
- How did the Lord react to that? He took back His forgiveness and put the unforgiving servant in jail.

•19•
Goals

"Press Forward, Saints" (*Hymns*, 81)
"Nephi's Courage" (*Children's Songbook*, 120)

 Scripture memory: Mark 9:23

 Activity 1: Mark 9:23
- How many things are possible? All things.
- Why are they possible? Through hope and faith.
- What kinds of goals should you set? Anything good that you want. God can help you do anything.
- How will you accomplish those goals? With God's help, work, and diligence.

 Activity 2: 1 Nephi 3:7
- What did Nephi say he would do? Obey the commandments.
- Why was he so confident? He knew God wouldn't command him to do anything that was impossible.
- God gives us commandments, and sometimes they

are hard to obey. But if we try our best and set goals, we can do anything.

 ### Activity 3: Genesis 6:14–22

- What did Noah have to do? Build a giant ark to save the animals during the flood.
- Does that sound like an easy job? No. It was hard and took a long time.
- How did Noah do it? He had God's help. He was commanded, so he did it.

 ### Activity 4: Galatians 6:7

- What things do you reap? Only the things you sow.
- Will you reach your goal if you do nothing? No. You must practice and study and pray often to reach your goals. Every action or inaction has an effect.

 ### Activity 5: James 1:22–25

- What does a hearer do? He only hears but doesn't put the lesson into practice.
- What does a doer do? He lives the gospel and is obedient.
- Why should you set goals? To improve and to help you become a doer instead of just a hearer.

•20•
Gratitude

"Count Your Blessings" (Hymns, 241)
"A Song of Thanks" (Children's Songbook, 20)

▶ *Scripture memory: D&C 78:19*

★ *Activity 1: Alma 34:38*
- What does it mean to live in thanksgiving daily? Have an attitude of gratitude all the time. Give thanks every day to everyone who helps or blesses you.
- What should you give thanks for? Mercies and blessings God has given us.

🔍 *Activity 2: Mosiah 2:20–21*
- When have we given enough thanks? We never can, even if we are always giving thanks with every breath.
- Why can't we thank enough? Because God gives us every breath, every comfort that we have, our ability to move and make choices.

Activity 3: D&C 78:19

• What happens when you are grateful? You will be made glorious.

• Will you get more or fewer blessings? You get more blessings, one hundred-fold more.

• When you are always wishing you had something you can't have, how do you feel? Sad. When you are busy being grateful, you don't have time to be sad.

Activity 4: Luke 17:11–19

• Who did Jesus heal? The ten lepers.

• How many came back to thank Him? Only one came back to thank Him.

• How much are we thankful? Only one-tenth as much as we should be.

Activity 5: Ether 6:5–12

• Who crossed the ocean? The Brother of Jared and his people.

• Was the journey easy? No. It was very long and difficult.

• What did they do when they reached the Promised Land? They bowed down and shed tears of joy that the Lord had been so merciful to them.

• How can we show our gratitude to the Lord and others? By thanking, praying, singing, and helping others.

•21•
Holy Ghost

"Let the Holy Spirit Guide" (*Hymns,* 143)
"The Holy Ghost" (*Children's Songbook,* 105)

 Scripture memory: Moroni 10:5

 Activity 1: D&C 130:22

• Does the Holy Ghost have a body? No, he is a personage of spirit.

• What can the Holy Ghost do? Dwell in us, help us know right from wrong, give us courage.

Activity 2: D&C 33:15

• How does someone get the Holy Ghost? By the laying on of hands.

• What do you have to do first? Be baptized and confirmed a member of the Church.

⭐ Activity 3: 2 Nephi 32:5; Moroni 10:5

* What does the Holy Ghost show you? The things you should do.

* How can you know the truth of all things? Through the Holy Ghost.

🧩 Activity 4: Helaman 4:24; Moroni 8:25–26

* Why did the Holy Ghost cease to dwell with the Nephites? Because they were wicked, the Holy Ghost couldn't dwell with them and strengthen them.

* What are unholy temples? They are people who do not keep themselves holy. They aren't holy because they are sinning or are too proud.

* What do we need to do to have the Holy Ghost with us? Repent and be humble.

* What does the Holy Ghost fill us with? Comfort, love, and hope.

🔤 Activity 5: Mosiah 5:1–2

* How did the people's hearts change? Through the power of the Holy Ghost. If we want to change our hearts, the Holy Ghost can help us.

•22•
Honesty

"Choose the Right" (*Hymns*, 239)
"I Believe in Being Honest" (*Children's Songbook*, 149)

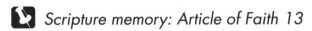 Scripture memory: Article of Faith 13

 Activity 1: Genesis 4:8–10; Exodus 20:16
- Did Cain really not know where Abel was? No. Cain knew he had murdered Abel.
- Was God fooled by his lie? No. God knows everything.
- What does it mean to bear false witness? It means to not be truthful.
- A lie is any communication given to another with the intent to deceive.

Activity 2: Acts 5:1–10
- What did Ananias and Sapphira do that was not honest? They tried to cheat the Lord out of money.

- What happened to them? They died.
- Will every lie make you fall down dead? No. But when we lie, we do spiritually die inside.
- If you cheat to win something, what do you lose? Your honor.

 Activity 3: Article of Faith 13

- What kinds of things should we seek? Honesty, truth, chastity, benevolence, virtue, etc.
- What does it mean to seek those things? Support people with those virtues, seek opportunities to improve, and develop those characteristics in ourselves.
- Why do you think honesty is listed first? It is hard to have any of the other virtues if you are not honest.

Activity 4: Joseph Smith–History 1:24–25

- The people in Joseph Smith's town wanted him to deny he saw a vision. Did he deny it? No. He knew it was true and could not deny it.
- Should we change our story if people don't believe the truth? No. We should always tell the truth.

Activity 5: 2 Nephi 28:7–9

- It is okay to lie a little? No. Little lies lead to bigger lies. Many people lie to cover up their mistakes, but it is better to admit our shortcomings and repent.

•23•
Honor Parents

"Home Can Be a Heaven on Earth" (*Hymns,* 298)
"Love Is Spoken Here" (*Children's Songbook,* 190)

▶ *Scripture memory: Exodus 20:12*

▦ *Activity 1: 1 Nephi 1:1*
- What did Nephi think of his parents? They were goodly.
- Do you think he honored them? Yes, because he obeyed their teachings.
- What did his parents do for him? They taught him and helped him.
- How can you honor your parents? Say good things about them, listen to them, be grateful for what they do for you.

★ *Activity 2: Exodus 20:12*
- This is part of the Ten Commandments. What does it say you should do to your father and mother? Honor them.

- How should you honor them? Obey, help, and respect them.
- What is the promise if you obey this? You will live long in the land.
- Why do you think you will live long in the land? Because your parents teach you to be safe and to take care of yourself and be responsible.

🔤 Activity 3: Alma 56:45–48
- Why were the stripling warriors so brave? They believed in the power of God.
- Who taught them to believe in the power of God? Their mothers.
- What can make you strong? If you listen to your parents, have faith.

🧩 Activity 4: D&C 19:24
- Did Jesus honor His Father? Yes.
- How do we know He honored His Father? He was obedient and did God's will.
- How can we honor our father? By being obedient, loving, helpful, and respectful.

❓ Activity 5: 1 Nephi 16:18–25
- What happened after Nephi broke his bow? They couldn't get food and everyone began complaining.
- Did Nephi take charge? No. He went to his father.

- How did this honor his father? It showed Nephi still respected his father, even though Lehi was murmuring. It helped his father regain his faith.

•24•
Humility

"In Humility, Our Savior" (*Hymns,* 172)
"When He Comes Again" (*Children's Songbook,* 82)

 Scripture memory: Matthew 18:3

 Activity 1: Ether 12:23–27

- What weakness did Moroni have? He was not very good at writing.
- What did the Lord say to comfort him? Your weaknesses make you strong because they humble you.
- What can weaknesses become? They can become your strengths if you let the Lord help you.

 Activity 2: Luke 18:9–14

- How did the Pharisee pray? He boasted of all the good deeds he had done.
- How did the publican pray? He recognized that he was a sinner. He asked for forgiveness. He was humble.
- Who will be exalted? The one who was humble.

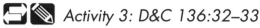 *Activity 3: D&C 136:32–33*

- How does a person learn wisdom? By humbling himself and calling upon God.

- When you are humble, who helps you learn? The Holy Spirit.

Activity 4: Matthew 18:1–4

- Who is the greatest in the kingdom of heaven? The little children.

- Why are they the greatest? Because they are innocent, humble, and teachable.

Activity 5: Alma 32:12–16

- Why were these people humble? They had been cast out of their churches; they were poor.

- What happens when someone is compelled (forced) to be humble? They seek God and repentance.

- Is it better to be compelled to be humble, or to be humble naturally? It is better to be humble without being compelled.

•25•
Israel

"Israel, Israel, God Is Calling" (*Hymns*, 7)
"The Tenth Article of Faith" (*Children's Songbook*, 128)

 Scripture memory: Article of Faith 10

 Activity 1: Genesis 32:28

- Who was Israel? Jacob the patriarch.
- Who was Jacob? He was the son of Isaac, who was the son of Abraham.
- Why did the Lord call Jacob Israel? Because Jacob would be a prince and the father of many nations.

 *Activity 2: Joshua 4:4, 8*

- How many tribes of Israel were there? Twelve.
- What were some of their names? Reuben, Simeon, Levi, Judah, Issachar, Zebulun, Dan, Naphtali, Gad, Asher, Joseph, and Benjamin.

- Where did the twelve tribes come from? They are the descendants of the twelve sons of Israel.

🔠 Activity 3: 1 Nephi 10:12

- What would happen to the house of Israel? They would be scattered like the branches of an olive tree.
- What does being scattered mean? They are living in many different nations instead of in Jerusalem.

🧩 Activity 4: D&C 110:11

- Who appeared to Joseph Smith? Moses.
- What did Moses do? He gave Joseph the key of the gathering of the twelve tribes of Israel. Missionary work is a way of gathering Israel. Everyone who is a member of the Church is a member of the house of Israel.

❓ Activity 5: Article of Faith 10

- What is the "literal" gathering of Israel? The descendants of Israel gathering to live and worship together.
- Is that happening? Yes. Many people are being gathered to the Church who are of the house of Israel.

•26•
Joseph Smith

"Praise to the Man" (*Hymns*, 27)
"On a Golden Springtime" (*Children's Songbook*, 88)

 *Scripture memory: Joseph Smith–History 1:17*

Activity 1: Joseph Smith–History 1:11–13

• What did Joseph Smith think about James 1:5? He knew he had to pray about which church is true.

• Why couldn't the Bible answer his questions? Everyone interpreted it differently; he needed more help.

Activity 2: Joseph Smith–History 1:17–19

• Who did Joseph Smith see after he prayed? He saw two personages.

• Who were the personages? They were Heavenly Father and Jesus.

• What did Joseph Smith ask? Which church he should join.

- What did they tell Joseph Smith? That all the churches were wrong and that he shouldn't join any of them.

📋 Activity 3: Joseph Smith–History 1:25
- What happened when Joseph Smith told people about his vision? They wouldn't believe him, and they persecuted him.
- Did the persecution make him doubt what he saw? No. He could not deny what he had seen.

📖 Activity 4: Joseph Smith–History 1:30–34
- Joseph continued to pray. After a few years, what happened? The angel Moroni appeared to him.
- What did Moroni tell him? He told him about the gold plates.
- What did the gold plates have written on them? The history of ancient Americans and the fullness of the gospel.

❓ Activity 5: D&C 135:1–3
- What happened in Carthage Jail? Joseph and Hyrum were killed.
- How were they killed? They were shot by an angry mob.
- Why were they martyrs? Because they were killed for their testimonies of Jesus.

•27•
Millennium

"Now Let Us Rejoice" (Hymns, 3)
"When He Comes Again" (Children's Songbook, 82)

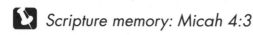 *Scripture memory: Micah 4:3*

Activity 1: Article of Faith 10

• When will Christ reign personally upon the earth? In the Millennium.

• What is paradisaical glory? The earth will be a paradise as it was in the garden of Eden.

• How long is the Millennium? One thousand years.

Activity 2: Micah 4:1–3

• What is the mountain that Micah talks about? A symbol for the temple.

• What will happen to their swords and spears? They will be fashioned into tools for peace.

• How will the people behave? They will walk in the name of the Lord; they will be righteous.

- When will all this happen? When Jesus reigns, in the Millennium.

🧩 Activity 3: 1 Nephi 22:26

- What will happen to Satan during the Millennium? He will be bound.
- Why will Satan be bound? Because people will be so righteous, they won't listen to him.

❓ Activity 4: D&C 101:30–34

- What are some of the great things that will happen during the Millennium? There will be no sorrow, and we will learn things that haven't yet been revealed.
- Will people be buried in the earth? No, when they die, they will be instantly resurrected.

⭐ Activity 5: D&C 45:55–59

- What parable will be fulfilled? The parable of the ten virgins.
- How will it be fulfilled? The wise ones will be prepared for Christ's coming.
- In what way will they be prepared? They will have received the truth and followed the Spirit.
- What will be their reward? They can live during the Millennium, multiply and be strong, and have children that grow up without sin.
- Where will the Lord be? On the earth, in their midst.

•28•
Miracles

"Master, the Tempest Is Raging" (Hymns, 105)
"My Heavenly Father Loves Me" (Children's Songbook, 228)

 Scripture memory: 2 Nephi 27:23

 Activity 1: D&C 35:8–10
- Who will see signs and miracles? Those who believe.
- What sorts of miracles can be done in faith? Healing the sick, casting out devils, restoring sight to the blind, healing deafness, making the lame walk.
- How is this possible? Through faith and the power of the priesthood.

 Activity 2: Mormon 9:16–20
- What are some of God's miracles? He made the earth, He created man.
- Who else did many mighty miracles? Jesus and the Apostles.

- Is God still a God of miracles? Yes. He has not changed.
- Why don't people see as many miracles today? They don't have enough faith.

 ### Activity 3: Ether 12:12–18
- What do people need to have before God can show a miracle? They must have faith.
- Who was able to perform miracles and what were they? Ammon and Amulek caused the prison walls to fall, Nephi and Lehi brought the Holy Ghost to the Lamanites, Ammon was able to bring the gospel to the Lamanites.

 ### Activity 4: Helaman 10:12–13
- Nephi did a great miracle for the people. Did that help them believe the gospel? No. They still hardened their hearts.
- Will a miracle give someone faith? No. Faith must come before the miracle.

 ### Activity 5: James 5:14–15
- What do you do if you need a miracle? You can call the elders of the Church.
- Why should you call them? They have the priesthood, which is the power to do miracles in Jesus' name.
- What will the elders do? Pray for the person and anoint him.

•29•
Missionary Work

"Called to Serve" (*Hymns*, 249)
"I Hope They Call Me on a Mission" (*Children's Songbook*, 169)

 Scripture memory: D&C 18:15

 Activity 1: D&C 18:15–16

• Why would someone labor so long in order to teach one person the gospel? Because helping even one soul will bring great joy.

• What will cause even greater joy? Bringing many souls to Christ. Missionary work is bringing souls to God.

⭐ *Activity 2: Matthew 28:19–20*

• Who did Jesus send the disciples to teach? All nations.

• What did He want them to teach? His gospel.

• Then what were they supposed to do? Baptize them.

Activity 3: Alma 17:6–11

- What did the sons of Mosiah give up to go on their mission to the Lamanites? The kingship, comfort, and security.
- What did they endure? Suffering and persecution.
- What did they need in order to be an instrument in the hands of the Lord? They needed His Spirit.

Activity 4: Alma 26:27–31

- What did they suffer at the hands of the Lamanites because they wanted to teach them the gospel? They were mocked, stoned, spat upon, and cast into prison.
- Why did they agree to do this? In order to save the souls of these people—even one of them.
- How many people did they help? Many people learned about the gospel and were converted through their efforts.

Activity 5: D&C 4

- Who is called to the work? Those who desire to serve the Lord.
- What is ready to harvest? People who are ready to hear the gospel.
- What happens to those who work with their might? They bring salvation to their souls.
- What qualifies someone for the work? Faith, hope, charity, love, and loyalty to God.

•30•
Music

"Come, Sing to the Lord" (*Hymns,* 10)
"Lift Up Your Voice and Sing" (*Children's Songbook,* 252)

🔖 *Scripture memory: D&C 25:12*

📖 *Activity 1: D&C 25:11–12*

- This counsel was given to Emma Smith. What was she told to compile? A collection of hymns.
- How does the Lord feel about a song of the heart? He delights in it.
- How does the Lord view the song of the righteous? It is the same as a prayer, and He will bless us for it.

🔍 *Activity 2: 1 Chronicles 15:15–16*

- What were the children of Israel doing? Moving the ark of the covenant.
- Why did they have the instruments and singers going

before? To praise God, to ask God's help in moving the ark, to thank God for His goodness, to show their joy.

Activity 3: D&C 136:28

- What can we use to praise the Lord? Singing, music, and dancing.
- What should accompany the singing and dancing? A prayer of thanksgiving.

Activity 4: Moroni 6:9

- How did the Nephites decide what to do in their meetings? They listened to the Spirit.
- What were some things the Spirit might direct them to do? Preach, exhort, pray, supplicate, or sing.
- Is singing in church a new practice? No. The Nephites and ancient Israelites also sang.

Activity 5: Exodus 15:19–21

- What had just happened to Pharaoh's armies? They had been washed away in the sea.
- Why did Miriam begin singing and dancing? Because she was so happy with what the Lord had done for Israel. She was celebrating.

•31•
Obedience

"Keep the Commandments" (*Hymns*, 303)
"Nephi's Courage" (*Children's Songbook*, 120)

🔖 *Scripture memory: 1 Nephi 3:7*

🔲 *Activity 1: 1 Nephi 3:1–7*

• Is it possible to be obedient to all of God's command-ments? Yes. He will not give us anything that is too hard to do.

• What did the Lord tell Lehi in a dream? That Lehi's sons should go back to Jerusalem to get the brass plates from Laban.

• What did Lamen and Lemuel think of this? They mur-mured that it would be too hard.

• Did Nephi complain? No. He had faith and was ready to obey.

? *Activity 2: Alma 57:18–22*

• What kind of soldiers were the sons of Helaman? They obeyed every command exactly and bravely.

• How were they able to fight so well? They had faith the Lord would help them.

• Why did they win the battle? They were obedient soldiers and brave.

• How will we win our battles in life? By obeying the commandments and by listening to the Spirit.

🔳 *Activity 3: Ephesians 6:1*

• Who should children obey? They should obey their parents.

• When should they obey their parents? When they are "in the Lord."

• What does "in the Lord" mean? They are being righteous and being good examples.

ABC *Activity 4: D&C 130:20–21*

• How do we get a blessing? By obeying the commandments. We can't be blessed with good health if we abuse our body. We can't be blessed with safety if we are reckless. We can't be guided by the Spirit if we refuse to fast and pray and meditate. We can't learn anything if we don't study.

Activity 5: Genesis 22:9–13, 18

- What was Abraham about to do? Go up the mountain and sacrifice his only son.

- Was Abraham willing to do it? Yes. He was about to sacrifice Isaac when the angel stopped him.

- What was Abraham's blessing for being faithful? He would have a great number of descendents. He would also receive other great blessings.

•32•
Ordinances

"Hark, All Ye Nations!" (*Hymns*, 264)
"Third Article of Faith" (*Children's Songbook*, 123)

📖 *Scripture memory: Article of Faith 3*

⭐ *Activity 1: Article of Faith 3*
- How are all mankind saved? Through the atonement of Christ and the ordinances of the gospel.
- What are the ordinances of the gospel? Baptism, receiving the Holy Ghost, ordination to the priesthood, temple ordinances, and the sacrament.

🔄 *Activity 2: D&C 124:33*
- What ordinance is talked about in this verse? Baptism for the dead.
- Where does that ordinance have to take place? In the temple.
- What other ordinances have to take place in a special

place? Ordinances for the dead, endowment, and temple marriage have to be performed in the temple.

 Activity 3: D&C 1:13–16

• What is one thing that displeases the Lord? When people stray from the ordinances and break their covenants.

• When people seek not the Lord, what do they do? Walk in their own way—use their own ideas instead of following God's plan.

• How do we know the correct ordinances? The Lord restored them to earth through the Prophet Joseph Smith.

 Activity 4: D&C 84:19–22

• How is the power of godliness manifest? Through the ordinances.

• Why is the priesthood necessary? If not performed under proper authority, the ordinances aren't acceptable to the Lord.

• Can you see God and live? Only if you have the ordinances.

 Activity 5: D&C 138:29–34

• What happens if you die without receiving the ordinances? You can have your ordinances done for you.

• Where must these ordinances be performed for someone who has died? In the temple.

•33•
Patience

"God Speed the Right" (*Hymns*, 106)
"Kindness Begins with Me" (*Children's Songbook*, 145)

📖 *Scripture memory: James 1:19–20*

🔤 *Activity 1: 1 Thessalonians 5:14*
- What is patience? Not being mad when things don't go your way or being willing to wait for something.
- What should you do to the unruly? Warn them.
- What should you do to the slow or weak? Help them, don't judge them or get angry with them.

📖 *Activity 2: Mosiah 24:9–15*
- What did Amulon do to Alma's people? He made them his slaves and gave them hard tasks to do.
- What did Alma's people do? They prayed for help, and God strengthened them.

• How did they bear their burdens? With patience and cheerfulness.

🎛 Activity 3: Hebrews 12:1–2

• What is the race set before us? The experiences of life.

• How should we run that race? With patience.

• What makes it possible to be patient in our afflictions? Our faith in Jesus.

❓🖊 Activity 4: James 1:19–20

• What should you be swift to do? Hear the word of the Lord.

• What should you be slow to do? Speak harshly or get angry.

• Why should you be this way? So you can do righteousness.

🔡 Activity 5: Alma 34:40–41

• Sometimes people are mean to you. Why shouldn't you be mean back? Because then you are just like they are.

• If our afflictions are great, should we lose hope? No. Because someday we will rest from all troubles; they will not go on forever.

•34•
Peacemaker

"Where Can I Turn for Peace?" (*Hymns*, 129)
"Love One Another" (*Children's Songbook*, 136)

⚡ *Scripture memory: Matthew 5:9*

⭐ *Activity 1: Matthew 5:9*
- Who is blessed in this verse? The peacemakers.
- What are peacemakers? They help others feel peace.
- What are they also called? The children of God.
- Why are they called the children of God? Because they are behaving like Jesus, who brings us all peace.

🔄 *Activity 2: Matthew 5:43–46*
- What does the world teach? Love your neighbors and hate your enemies.
- What did Jesus teach? Love your enemies also. If you take offense from or seek revenge on people who curse, persecute, and hate you, you will cause fights, not peace.
- How can you make peace? Pray for your enemies, do

good to them. It is easy to love those who love you, but we are to love everyone.

Activity 3: Luke 6:35–38

- Who are our enemies? They may be people that we don't understand or someone we have a quarrel with.
- How does Heavenly Father treat people who are not thankful? He is kind to them.

Activity 4: Matthew 5:25

- When should you agree with your enemy? While you are in the way with him.
- Is it better to resolve the conflict sooner or later? Sooner.
- Why? Then other people don't have to get involved.

Activity 5: Isaiah 9:6

- What is one of Jesus' names that has to do with peace? The Prince of Peace.
- Why is he called the Prince of Peace? He can give us peace if we are angry or scared or confused.
- Why should we try to make peace? So we can be like Jesus.

•35•
Pioneers

"Come, Come, Ye Saints" (*Hymns*, 30)
"Pioneer Children Sang as They Walked" (*Children's Songbook*, 214)

OH=Our Heritage: A Brief History of The Church of Jesus Christ of Latter-day Saints

📖 *Scripture memory: D&C 45:66*

📖 *Activity 1: 1 Nephi 2:20 and D&C 45:66*

• Where was the Lord going to lead Nephi? To a land of promise.

• How is this land of promise described in 1 Nephi? Prepared, choice above all other lands.

• How is this land of promise described for the Mormon pioneers in D&C? "A land of peace, a city of refuge, a place of safety for the saints of the Most High God."

🔲 Activity 2: OH, p. 69, "The Trials of a Winter Trek"; D&C Stories, chapter 60

- What were some of the trials that the pioneers had to go through? They had to leave in the middle of winter, cross the Mississippi River, live in tents, and do without food.

🔲 Activity 3: OH, p. 71, "Winter Quarters"; D&C Stories, chapter 62

- What was Winter Quarters? A temporary town where the Saints prepared for their journey west.

- Who would harvest the crops that were planted in Winter Quarters? The pioneers who came later.

- How did the pioneers get though their trials? By exercising faith.

❓ Activity 4: OH, p. 74, "The Brooklyn Saints"

- Where did the *Brooklyn* go? From the east coast of the United States to California by sea.

- Who was on the *Brooklyn*? About 300 men, women, and children.

- Did the voyage go smoothly? No. They had bad food, storms, and sickness to contend with.

📖 Activity 5: OH, p. 77, "Handcart Pioneers"; D&C Stories, chapter 64

- What did the handcart pioneers do? They pulled a cart by hand. It contained only a few supplies.

- How well did the handcart companies manage? Eight did well, but two had problems. The Willie and Martin handcart companies got caught in early winter storms.

- Did their suffering make them bitter? No. Survivors stayed very strong in the faith because they had come to know the Savior.

•36•
Plan of Salvation

"'Tis Sweet to Sing the Matchless Love" (*Hymns,* 177)
"I Lived in Heaven" (*Children's Songbook,* 4)

 *Scripture memory: 2 Nephi 2:25*

 *Activity 1: Abraham 3:22–25; D&C 93:29*
- What did the Lord show Abraham? Intelligences that existed before the world was created.
- Who was with God in the beginning? Man was with God.
- What did the Lord make the earth for? To test man.

Activity 2: 2 Nephi 2:24–26
- Why did Adam fall? So that men could be.
- What are men supposed to do? Have joy, eternal life.
- What is the Messiah going to do? Come in the fullness of time to redeem His people.
- What does it mean to be free? To be able to choose your own path.

- Does that mean there are no consequences? No. You still have to obey the laws.

⮌🖎 *Activity 3: D&C 76:40–42*

- What makes the plan of salvation possible? The atonement of Jesus Christ.
- What did His sacrifice do for the world? It cleansed the world from unrighteousness. Because He died for us, we can be saved from death and sin and live with Him again.

🔍 *Activity 4: Alma 40:11–14*

- Between death and resurrection, where does your spirit go? Back to dwell with God, to a place called paradise, where you will rest from care.
- Who will be in paradise? The good spirits.
- Why do the bad spirits suffer? Because they don't have a portion of the Spirit of the Lord, and the devil has control of them.

⮌ *Activity 5: D&C 76: 69–70, 71–76, 81–82, 111*

- v. 111. How are people judged? According to their works.
- vv. 81–82. What is the telestial kingdom likened to? The glory of the stars, no gospel of Christ, no testimony of Jesus.
- vv. 71–76. What is the terrestrial kingdom likened to? The glory of the moon, for those who died without the law

but received the testimony of Jesus later, those who were honorable but deceived.

- vv 69–70. Who will go to the celestial kingdom? Those made perfect through Jesus' atonement. They are likened to the glory of the sun.

•37•
Prayer

"Did You Think to Pray?" (*Hymns*, 140)
"We Bow Our Heads" (*Children's Songbook*, 25)

 Scripture memory: 3 Nephi 18:20

 *Activity 1: 2 Nephi 32:9*
- When should you pray? Always.
- Why should you pray before performing anything? So the Lord will consecrate it and it will be for the good of your soul.
- What does it mean to "perform something"? Anything you might do, not just things you do in front of people.
- What are some things that you might pray about before doing?

Activity 2: Matthew 6:9–13
- What is Jesus teaching here? How to pray.
- What should we ask for? Daily bread or sustenance, protection from evil and temptation, forgiveness.

- Who should we give glory to? The Father.

▦ Activity 3: Luke 18:10–14

- How did the Pharisee pray? To be seen of other men, to show off.
- How did the publican pray? He was humble and he asked for forgiveness.
- How should we pray? We should be humble and thankful.

❓ Activity 4: Alma 34:20–27

- Where can you pray? Anywhere: in fields, houses, closets.
- When should you pray? Morning, midday, and evening.
- What should you pray for? Your work, your family, your welfare, power against the devil.

▦ Activity 5: James 1:5–6

- How can you gain wisdom? You can ask God in prayer.
- Do you only need to ask? No. You also have to have faith.
- Does God help only some people? No. He will help all who have faith to ask Him.

•38•
Preparation

"I Have Work Enough to Do" (*Hymns*, 224)
"We'll Bring the World His Truth" (*Children's Songbook*, 172)

📖 *Scripture memory: Alma 34:32*

⭐ *Activity 1: D&C 109:8*
- What should you prepare? Every needful thing.
- What is every needful thing? Prepare for the things you will need spiritually, temporally, and physically. Those things don't happen by accident. Your life will be much more comfortable if you are prepared with the things you will need.

❓ *Activity 2: Alma 43:19–21*
- Which of the armies were better prepared? The Nephites. They had better armor to protect themselves.
- How did the Lamanites react when they saw how the Nephites had prepared? They were afraid to fight them.

- What will help us conquer our foes? We should prepare as best as we can.

◻✎ Activity 3: Alma 12:24
- What is man to do with the space granted him by God? Prepare to meet God.
- How do you prepare to meet God? By repenting.

🔍 Activity 4: Alma 34:32–33
- What do we need to do in this life? Prepare to meet God.
- Why can't we put it off for tomorrow? We shouldn't procrastinate because we never know how much time we will have.
- What can we do while on earth that we can't do after death? We can't perform labor after death, so we should labor while we can.

📋 Activity 5: D&C 133:4–10
- How did the Lord ask these people to prepare? Be clean, gather together to help and strengthen each other, do missionary work.
- Who is the bridegroom? Jesus Christ.
- When the bridegroom comes it will be a great day. Why do we need to prepare? So we can be ready to see God and not have anything to be ashamed of.

•39•
Priesthood

"Ye Elders of Israel" (*Hymns,* 319)
"A Young Man Prepared" (*Children's Songbook,* 166)

N *Scripture memory: D&C 121:41*

? *Activity 1: D&C 107:1–10*
- What are the two priesthoods in the Church? Aaronic and Melchizedek.
- Why is the first called the Melchizedek Priesthood? Out of respect for the name of the Supreme Being.
- What are things that the Melchizedek Priesthood has authority over? Presidency, spiritual things, and the right to officiate in Church offices and to preside over the Levitical (Aaronic) Priesthood.

▦ *Activity 2: D&C 107:13, 14, 20*
- What is the power and authority of the Aaronic Priesthood? The power to administer in the outward ordinances.

- Why is it called the "lesser priesthood?" Because it is only a part of the Melchizedek Priesthood.

🔲 Activity 3: D&C 84:6–17

- Where did Moses get the priesthood? From his father-in-law, Jethro.
- Where did Jethro get the priesthood? He got it from other priesthood holders all the way back to Adam, who was the first man.
- Is there a time when the Church will not have the priesthood? No. The Church will always have the priesthood in it.

🔲 Activity 4: D&C 84:20–26

- How do we see the power of God? Through the ordinances. If we didn't have the priesthood, the ordinances wouldn't work.
- What did Moses want his people to do? Be sanctified so they could see God.
- Did the children of Israel cooperate? No. They rebelled and the greater priesthood was taken from them.
- Did they have any priesthood left? Yes. They retained the lesser priesthood for officiating in the outward ordinances of the preparatory gospel.

🔲 Activity 5: D&C 121:41–43

- Can someone with the priesthood do whatever he

wants and still have power? No. Priesthood holders must remain righteous.

- How should a priesthood holder influence people? Through long-suffering, gentleness, meekness, and love.

•40•
Restoration

"The Spirit of God" (*Hymns*, 2)
"On a Golden Springtime" (*Children's Songbook*, 88)

 Scripture memory: Revelation 14:6

 Activity 1: 1 Nephi 13:25–27

- What happened to the plain and precious parts of the gospel? They were taken away.

- Why did the evil men do this? To blind the eyes and harden the hearts of men.

 Activity 2: Isaiah 29:13–14

- Who did men trust after the gospel was lost? They trusted the wisdom of men. They didn't have the light of the gospel to lead them any more.

- Was God going to do anything about it? Yes. He was going to work a marvelous work and a wonder.

- What is that "marvelous work and a wonder"? The

restoration of the gospel, especially the translation of the Book of Mormon.

 Activity 3: D&C 128:20–21

• What happened at Cumorah? Joseph Smith saw the angel Moroni and was shown the gold plates, which started the events of the Restoration.

• Who were some of the other angels who came to restore the gospel? Some of the angels were Peter, James, and John; John the Baptist; and many others.

• What did these angels bring? The keys and rights of their priesthood authority.

 Activity 4: Daniel 2:44

• What is the kingdom that will never be destroyed? The kingdom of God or the Church that was restored to the earth.

• Will the gospel ever be taken away again? No.

 Activity 5: Revelation 14:6

• Who is going to get to hear the gospel? Every nation, kindred, tongue, and people.

• What does "every nation, kindred, tongue, and people" mean? Everyone.

•41•
Resurrection

"Christ the Lord Is Risen Today" (*Hymns*, 200)
"Did Jesus Really Live Again?" (*Children's Songbook*, 64)

 Scripture memory: 1 Corinthians 15:22

 Activity 1: 1 Corinthians 15:20–22
- What happened because of Adam? All men have to die someday.
- Will everyone be resurrected? Yes.
- Who made it possible for everyone to be resurrected? Christ made it possible for everyone to be resurrected.

 Activity 2: Acts 26:23; Luke 24:36–43
- Who was the first to be resurrected? Christ was the first person resurrected.
- What were some things Jesus did after He was resurrected? He visited his disciples. He let them touch His hands and feet. He ate fish and honeycomb with them.

- Why did He eat with them? To show He had a physical body.

 ### Activity 3: D&C 76:89–98

- Is everyone resurrected to the same glory? No.
- What are the different glories called? Celestial, terrestrial, telestial.

 ### Activity 4: D&C 88:14–16

- The soul has two parts; what are they? The spirit and the body.
- Why is the resurrection the redemption of the soul? Because the spirit and the body are brought back together.
- How long will they remain joined? Forever.

Activity 5: D&C 130:18–19

- You can't take such things as money or possessions with you when you die. What do you take with you to the resurrection? Knowledge, intelligence, and relationships.
- How do you get intelligence in this life? Through diligence and obedience.

•42•
Revelation

"Let the Holy Spirit Guide" (*Hymns*, 143)
"Seek the Lord Early" (*Children's Songbook*, 108)

 Scripture memory: James 1:5

Activity 1: Amos 3:7

- If we are going to learn the secrets of God, what do we need? We need a prophet.

- What do prophets do? They receive revelation from the Lord for the Church.

Activity 2: James 1:5–6

- When you have a question and ask Heavenly Father for an answer, what are you asking for? Revelation.

- Can anyone receive revelation? Yes. If we ask with faith we will receive the knowledge we seek, which is the same as revelation.

Activity 3: 2 Nephi 28:30

- The Lord doesn't tell us everything at one time. How does He tell us things? Little by little.
- What happens if you listen to Him? He will give you more knowledge.
- What happens if you don't listen to Him? He will take away the knowledge you had.

 Activity 4: D&C 8:1–3

- What are some ways that you can receive revelation? In your mind and in your heart.
- What did Oliver Cowdery receive revelation about? How to translate.
- What can you receive revelation about? Whatever you need, if you have faith.
- Who needed revelation to bring the children of Israel out of Egypt? Moses.

 Activity 5: D&C 9:7–9

- What is another way you can know if something is right? You will feel a burning in your heart.
- Does it help to study things out? Yes. After you have done that, God will give you an answer or inspiration.
- Is it okay to ask without putting any thought into it? No. You have to put some effort in also.

•43•
Reverence

"Oh, May My Soul Commune with Thee"
(*Hymns*, 123)
"Reverently, Quietly" (*Children's Songbook*, 26)

[icon] *Scripture memory: D&C 76:93*

[icon] *Activity 1: D&C 76:92–93*
- What bows in reverence? All things bow to God.
- What is reverence? Showing respect, giving honor.
- How can we show reverence? By being quiet, folding our arms, bowing our heads, and closing our eyes during prayers.

[icon] *Activity 2: D&C 133:39–41*
- What is a blessing of reverence? If you are worshiping, you can feel the presence of the Lord.
- How do we worship the Lord? By giving praise, being obedient, praying, bowing, giving glory, being humble.

Activity 3: Psalms 111:9–10

- What does David call God's name? Holy and reverend.
- What does it mean to have the fear of the Lord? To honor, worship, and reverence Him.
- What does reverence lead to? Wisdom. It is hard to learn when it is noisy all around you or when you are proud.

Activity 4: 3 Nephi 11:13–17

- How would you feel if you saw Jesus appear?
- Why did the people fall to the earth? Some were frightened, others were respectful.
- How would you act if Jesus came to visit you? Respectful, humble.
- How should you act when you visit His house? Reverent.

Activity 5: Enos 1:4

- How did Enos show reverence? He knelt down.
- How can you show reverence?

•44•
Sabbath

"Welcome, Welcome, Sabbath Morning"
(*Hymns*, 280)
"Saturday" (*Children's Songbook*, 196)

○ *Scripture memory: Exodus 20:8*

★ *Activity 1: Exodus 20:8–11*
- How many days should we work? Six days.
- What do we do on the seventh day? Rest.
- What does "hallowed" mean? Something that is holy or sacred.
- What did God want the people of Israel to remember? That God created the world in six days and then rested on the seventh.

? *Activity 2: Exodus 16:14–27*
- What did the Israelites eat in the desert? Food from God called manna.

- When could they collect the manna? Everyday but Sunday.
- What did they eat on Sunday? Extra manna they had collected on Saturday.
- What can we do to prepare for Sunday? Wash our clothes, clean our houses, and shop on Saturday.

🔍 Activity 3: D&C 59:10–15

- How should you prepare your food on Sunday? With singleness of heart, nothing too complicated or hard to do.
- Should you be sad on the Sabbath because of the things you can't do? No. You should be thankful and cheerful.

🔄📝 Activity 4: D&C 59:9, 16–17

- What are the blessings you can have for keeping the Sabbath day holy? You will have plenty of food and plenty of clothes.
- What does it mean to be unspotted from the world? Free from sin, not worried about worldly things, more spiritual.

📋 Activity 5: Exodus 31:12–17

- In ancient Israel, what happened if the people didn't keep the Sabbath holy? They were put to death or banished.
- What does the covenant of the Sabbath show? Israel remembers what God has done for them.

•45•
Sacrament

"In Humility, Our Savior" (*Hymns,* 172)
"To Think about Jesus" (*Children's Songbook,* 71)

 Scripture memory: D&C 20:75

Activity 1: D&C 20:75–76
- What is the sacrament? When we take bread and water in remembrance of Jesus.
- When should we take the sacrament? We should take it often—every week.
- Who blesses the sacrament? The priests or Melchizedek Priesthood holders.

Activity 2: Luke 22:13–20
- What were the disciples eating? Passover. This special meal is called the "Last Supper."
- Why is it called the Last Supper? It would be the last time Jesus would eat before He died.

- What does the bread represent? His body.
- What does the cup represent? His blood.

Activity 3: 3 Nephi 18:1–11

- When the Nephites took the sacrament, what did it show Jesus? That they remembered Him.
- What does Jesus promise if you remember Him? That you can have His Spirit to be with you.
- Do you have to keep the commandments perfectly? No. But you must be willing to repent when you make a mistake.

Activity 4: Moroni 4:3

- What do we promise when we take the sacrament? That we are willing to take upon us Jesus' name, that we will always remember Him, and keep His commandments.
- What does Heavenly Father promise us? That we will always have His Spirit to be with us.

Activity 5: D&C 27:1–4

- Does it matter what you eat or drink during the sacrament? No. It only matters that you do so remembering Jesus' sacrifice for us.
- What are the important parts of the sacrament? Remembering Jesus and His body and blood that He gave for us and promising to be obedient to His commandments.

•46•
Sacrifice

"I'll Go Where You Want Me to Go" (*Hymns, 270*)
"The Church of Jesus Christ" (*Children's Songbook, 77*)

📖 *Scripture memory: 3 Nephi 9:20*

❓ *Activity 1: Moses 5:4–8*

• What did the angel tell Adam to do? Sacrifice the firstlings of his flocks unto God. Adam was obedient even though he didn't understand why.

• The angel explained why Adam needed to offer sacrifices. What did the angel say? It was to help Adam and his family think about how Jesus would be sacrificed for the sins of the world.

🔍 *Activity 2: Matthew 19:16–22*

• What did the rich young man ask Jesus? How he could have eternal life.

- What had the young man done? He had kept the commandments since his youth.

- What did he still need to do? He needed to sell all that he had and give to the poor and follow Jesus.

- Do you think he was going to do what Jesus asked? No. He was sad that he wasn't willing to make the needed sacrifice.

⭐ *Activity 3: Genesis 22:1–13*

- What did the Lord ask Abraham to sacrifice? His son.
- What stopped him? An angel stopped him.
- Was Abraham willing to give up his beloved son for the Lord? Yes.
- Why was Abraham willing to do such a thing? Because he loved and trusted the Lord.
- What was Abraham being taught? Abraham was being taught to look forward to and appreciate God's sacrifice of His Only Begotten Son to atone for the sins of the world.

📋 *Activity 4: 3 Nephi 9:19–20*

- Do we give burnt offerings to show our obedience anymore? No. The law of Moses was fulfilled by Christ's atonement.
- What kind of sacrifice do we need to give? A broken heart and a contrite spirit.

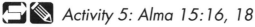 *Activity 5: Alma 15:16, 18*

- Sometimes we have to give more than a broken heart or contrite spirit for the Lord. Sometimes we have to give up other things. What did Amulek give up so he could be a member of God's church? He gave up his gold and precious things as well as his friends and family.

- Did giving up those things make Amulek sad? Maybe, but he was strengthened by Alma and the Lord.

•47•
Scriptures

"As I Search the Holy Scriptures" (*Hymns*, 277)
"Search, Ponder, and Pray" (*Children's Songbook*, 109)

▶ Scripture memory: 2 Nephi 4:15

▦ Activity 1: 1 Nephi 19:22–23
- Why did Nephi read the brass plates? So his people could know what the Lord had done among other people, so they could know the Savior, and so they could know where they came from.
- What prophets did Nephi read from? Moses and Isaiah.
- How do you liken the scriptures to yourself? You apply their teachings in your life. You can learn from the stories and examples they describe.

✎ Activity 2: Mosiah 1:3–7
- What would have happened if the people hadn't had the brass plates? They would have suffered in ignorance and

dwindled in unbelief because they would not have known the plan of salvation.

- How did they know that the records were true? They had them before their eyes.
- Why did the Lord want them to search the scriptures? So they could profit from them, grow in faith, and live the gospel.

Activity 3: D&C 1:37

- Where are the commandments written? They are written in the scriptures.
- Will the prophecies be fulfilled? Yes. All of them.
- Why should we study them? So we will know what is going to happen and be prepared.

Activity 4: 1 Nephi 5:21

- These records are the brass plates that Nephi got from Laban. Why were the scriptures of such great worth? The people could use them to remember the goodness of God and teach the gospel to their children.
- Are they of great worth to us? Yes. Without them we wouldn't know anything about God or His plan for us.

Activity 5: Psalms 119:105

- How are the scriptures a lamp and light? The scriptures show us the way we should go. If we didn't have the light, we would stumble in the darkness of ignorance.

•48•
Second Coming

"Now Let Us Rejoice" (*Hymns,* 3)
"When He Comes Again" (*Children's Songbook,* 82)

▶ *Scripture memory: Joseph Smith–Matthew 1:1*

▤ *Activity 1: Joseph Smith–Matthew 1:1*
- What is Jesus telling His disciples? That He will come again.
- How does He describe His Second Coming? He will come from the sky with His angels.
- How is that different than the first time He came? When He came the first time, He was born as a baby.

★ *Activity 2: Joseph Smith–Matthew 1:37–40*
- How do we know when the Second Coming is nearing? We watch for the signs.
- What is the parable of the fig tree? A reminder to watch for the signs of His coming. Just like when a fig tree grows new leaves, we know summer is coming.

- Does anyone know the exact time of the Second Coming? No one knows except Heavenly Father.

☝ Activity 3: Joseph Smith–Matthew 1:28–33

- What are some things that must happen before the Second Coming? Wars and rumors of wars, famines, earthquakes in many places, preaching the gospel to every nation, sun darkened, and the moon turned to blood.
- Who will be destroyed when Christ returns? The wicked will be destroyed.
- Why does God give us these signs? So we can be ready for the Second Coming by repenting and living good lives.

☝✎ Activity 4: D&C 29:11, 101:24–25

- What will happen to all the things that live on the earth? The corruptible things will be destroyed, everything will be new.
- Who will live on the earth then? Jesus will live here in glory with the righteous.
- How long will this last? One thousand years.

🔍 Activity 5: Article of Faith 10

- This article of faith describes some things that will be happening in the future. What are some of the things that will happen? The gathering of Israel, the building up of Zion, and the millennial reign of Christ. We should not be afraid because if we live righteously, everything will be fine.

•49•
Service

"Put Your Shoulder to the Wheel" (*Hymns,* 252)
"When We're Helping" (*Children's Songbook,* 198)

📖 *Scripture memory: Mosiah 2:17*

🔡 *Activity 1: Mosiah 2:14–18*

• Mosiah was the king. Did that stop him from serving people? No. He labored hard to make his own living and serve his subjects.

• Should you boast if you serve people? No.

• When you serve others, who do you also serve? God.

🔠 *Activity 2: Matthew 25:34–40*

• When did the righteous help the king? When they helped other people.

• What is their reward? They were to inherit the kingdom of God.

❓ Activity 3: Alma 34:27–29

- We should pray for those who are in need, but is that enough? No. We also need to help them.
- Why are you being a hypocrite if you don't help them? Because you are asking God to help, but you won't help.

📖 Activity 4: Luke 10:30–37

- Who wouldn't help the injured man? The priest and the Levite.
- Who helped the injured man? The Samaritan.
- How did the Samaritan help him? He gave the injured man food and clothes and tended his wounds and took him to an inn to be cared for.
- Which person truly loved his neighbor? How do you know that?

🔢 Activity 5: Proverbs 28:27

- If you give to the poor, what won't you lack? Things you need, especially spiritual things.
- What is the curse? Guilt and loss of the Spirit.

•50•
Talents

"Come, Let Us Anew" (*Hymns,* 217)
"Shine On" (*Children's Songbook,* 144)

📖 *Scripture memory: D&C 82:3*

❓ *Activity 1: Matthew 25:14–30*
- What could the talents represent? The ability to do things, our possessions.
- What are some kinds of talents? Musical, obedience, helping others, attitude, gifts of the Spirit.
- What did the servants in the parable do with their talents? Some increased them, some hid them.
- What should you do with your talents? You should work on the ones you have been given and try to increase them.

📋 *Activity 2: D&C 46:10–12*
- Does everyone have the same talents? No. There are many different gifts.

- Why doesn't everyone have the same talents? So everyone can share and be edified.
- Does everyone get a gift from God? Yes.

 ### Activity 3: D&C 60:2–3

- What happens if you don't use your talents? You will lose them.
- Why does that make God sad? It shows you don't appreciate His gift to you.

 ### Activity 4: D&C 82:3

- Some people have more talents than others; what are they expected to do? Those who have more will be required to do more.

 ### Activity 5: Matthew 5:14–16

- What is the candle in this verse? Our talents and example.
- What should we do with our candles? Let others see them; don't hide them.
- How should we use our talents? We should use our talents to bless our families and communities.

•51•
Tithing

"Because I Have Been Given Much" (Hymns, 219)
"I Want to Give the Lord My Tenth" (Children's Songbook, 150)

 Scripture memory: Malachi 3:10

 Activity 1: Alma 13:15

- Who paid tithes in this scripture? Abraham paid them to Melchizedek. Abraham lived a long time ago, so people have been paying tithing for a long time.
- Why did he pay them to Melchizedek? Because he was the high priest in the land.

Activity 2: Malachi 3:8–12

- How does a man rob God? If he doesn't pay his tithing and offerings.
- What is the blessing for paying tithing? God will open the windows of heaven and pour out blessings on the obedient.

- What are the windows of heaven? The source of all that God has, especially faith, increased Spirit, and revelation, along with material blessings.
- What is another blessing? The fruit of the ground (our crops) will not be destroyed. It will be a delightsome land.

★ Activity 3: D&C 64:23
- What does the Lord require of us? Sacrifice and tithing.
- What are tithe payers saved from? The burning at the Second Coming.

Activity 4: D&C 97:11–12
- What is tithing used for? Building temples and other Church buildings, printing and other expenses, missionary work, and ward budgets.
- What shouldn't it be spent on? Things that don't build the kingdom.

Activity 5: D&C 119:3–6
- How much is tithing? Ten percent of your annual income.
- How long will the tithing law stand? Forever.
- Do some tithing math.

•52•
Word of Wisdom

"In Our Lovely Deseret" (*Hymns*, 307)
"The Lord Gave Me a Temple" (*Children's Songbook*, 153)

📖 *Scripture memory: D&C 89:18*

❓ *Activity 1: D&C 89:1–4*

• What is the Word of Wisdom? Is it required? It is a commandment required of all Church members. You must obey the Word of Wisdom to be baptized or to enter the temple.

• Is this Word of Wisdom hard to keep? No. It is meant for even the weakest of all Saints.

• Why was the Word of Wisdom given? The Word of Wisdom teaches you how to help keep your body healthy. It also indicates our willingness to be obedient to the Lord.

Activity 2: D&C 89:4–9

- What is not good for man? Wine or strong drink, hot drinks, and tobacco.
- What are hot drinks? The prophets have said that these are coffee and tea.
- Does tobacco have any good uses? Yes. To treat bruises and sick cattle.

 Activity 3: D&C 89:10–17

- What things are good for man to eat? Herbs, fruits, and grains.
- What about flesh of beasts? They are okay, but only sparingly.

 Activity 4: D&C 89:18–21

- What are the blessings for keeping the Word of Wisdom? Health, wisdom, and strength and energy (run and not be weary). The destroying angel will also pass by the obedient.
- Are you only blessed with health? No. The Lord will also bless you with wisdom and hidden treasures of knowledge.

 Activity 5: Daniel 1:8–20

- What did the king want to feed Daniel and his friends? Rich food, meat, and wine.

- Did Daniel eat the food? No. He wanted only pulse (a grain dish) and water.
- How did Daniel talk the servant into letting them eat pulse and water? He told them to do an experiment.
- How did the experiment turn out? Daniel and his friends were the most healthy and wise of all the king's court.

How to Use the CD-ROM

All of the activities included on the CD-ROM are in .pdf format and will print exactly as they appear on the screen. *Note:* To print the activity sheets, you will need Adobe Reader software, which can be downloaded for free at the following website: www.adobe.com/products/acrobat/readstep2_allversions.html

Insert the enclosed CD-ROM into your CD drive. Once the Reader software begins, you will see the first page, which is the first activity for Agency. To see all six pages included for that topic, simply scroll or page down. If you want to see a list of all 52 topics, click the bookmark icon on the upper left-hand side of the screen (it looks like a page of lined paper with a blue ribbon in front of it). You can then click the topic of your choice.

Once you have selected a topic to print, simply click the printer icon and select either "Current page" to print only the page you have selected, or "Pages" to print a range of pages for the selected topic as listed in the table of contents; then type the page range. For example, if you wanted to print all the activities for the topic of Faith, you would click the printer icon, select "Pages," and enter 85-90.

Please note: All of the activities on the CD-ROM are for use by individual families or classes only. Printing or distributing the activities for any other use is prohibited.